The Colourful Life
Surprise Baby!

Naomi Kissiedu - Green

All rights reserved. No part of this book may be reproduced or transmitted in any form or by any means, electronic or mechanical, including photocopying, recording, or by an information storage and retrieval system - except by a reviewer who may quote brief passages in a review to be printed in a magazine or newspaper - without permission in writing from the publisher.

copyright © 2013. All rights reserved.
Naomi Kissiedu -Green
ISBN-13: 978-0994465627
ISBN-10: 0994465629

DEDICATION

I dedicate this book to my mother, Sylvia Laryea, who passed away before meeting my family. **I will always love you.**

To my Dad (Daddy), who raised myself and my siblings. You never stopped loving us. **You are my strength.**

To my husband, Matthew, children Kobi, Ebony and my soon to be baby, You give me so much **love and joy**.

Friends and family members who encourage me to take the plunge - you know who you are – and to them I offer my heartfelt gratitude.

And to all of you who have this book: **THANK YOU.**

NOTES FOR TEACHER OR PARENT

I write these books for children entering day care or pre-school who are becoming aware of the world outside of their families for the first time. They might notice things about people – like a baby growing inside a mother's "tummy" or someone's skin being different in hue from theirs. Since children are curious, they may ask, "What's in your tummy?" or "Why is my skin different from yours?"

I hope both parents and children are helped by the answers provided within my books.

When reading the stories, you may wish to ask your children about the identities depicted. Find out what your children's thoughts are about the different identities Exploring together the stories' scenarios will help children develop a better understanding of life's complexities and help them feel more settled and secure in themselves and their situation.

Surprise Baby

This is a story about a young boy called Kobi who is about to become a big brother. Kobi is very excited and can't wait to find out if the baby in his mummy's tummy will be a boy or a girl. Kobi learns what it's like to be a big brother and shares with his classmates the journey of his mummy's pregnancy.

ACKNOWLEDGMENTS

I would like to express my gratitude to the many people who helped to carry me through this book. To all those read, wrote, offered comments, and assisted in the editing, proofreading and illustrations, I offer my heartfelt gratitude.

And to my children, my darlings, I love you. You are my ultimate creations.

I am all things sweet, all things nice.

I am a bit of chocolate. I am a bit of vanilla.

I am a caramel delight.

It's my first day of kindergarten, and I am a little bit scared, but excited. Mummy kisses me goodbye and I let go of her hand. She waves at me and my new teacher Mrs. Laryea takes me to my classroom.

Inside, the classroom is very loud. Children are running around, finding their seats. Some kids are crying, having been dropped off and parents have left them, while others sit alone, too shy to speak. Suddenly, the noise stops and Mrs. Laryea steps in front of the class.

"Hello boys and girls, my name is Mrs. Laryea. Let's start today by saying our names and telling each other something wonderful that happened over the holidays. Let's start with you, Kobi." I am so excited that Mrs. Laryea picks me first. I get to tell the class about my new baby brother or sister that's coming.

Surprise Baby

"Hi, my name is Kobi and I am five years old. I live with my Mummy and Daddy. My mummy is pregnant and I am so excited! That means she is having a baby! Mummy's tummy is getting bigger and bigger. That's because the baby is growing inside her.

"In just a few days Mummy will have a baby and I will be a big brother. I don't know if I will have a baby brother or sister. It's going to be a super special surprise. Sometimes I sit on the sofa with Mummy and we talk to the baby. I tell the baby how excited I am to have someone to play with. I tell the baby I will share some of my toys with him or her, and that we will play games like hide-and-seek."

My classmates burst into laughter. One of them raises her hand. Her name is Emma. She asks me, "What do you think the baby will look
like? Do you think he'll be a boy like you?"

Then another classmate asks. "Do you think the new baby will have big curly hair like you, Kobi?"

My classmates ask me so many questions, that I become even more excited. I ask myself all the same things when I stare at Mommy's belly.

I can't wait until the baby arrives. Will my new sibling be taller than me? If it is a girl, will she play with dolls?

Will she want me to play with dolls too? And will she want to play dress-up?! I tell my classmates all the things I want to do with my new baby brother or sister.

The Big Day Is Here

The day I have been waiting for has finally arrived! I wake up extremely excited. I see the sun shining brightly through my window and I hear lots of chatter and shuffling around downstairs. My heart races like a sprinter running a race. I just know something magical is going to happen today!

Mummy comes into my bedroom. She tells me that my grandparents are downstairs and they are going to stay with me while Daddy and she head to the hospital. She says that I will see her very soon. She also tells me that my grandparents will be taking me to the hospital to see her and the new baby. Daddy and Mummy kiss me goodbye and head downstairs.

By the time my grandparents and I arrive at the hospital, I am bursting with excitement. I walk quickly through the hospital corridors impatient to find my mother. I can hardly wait! Finally we find the right room. When we enter, Mummy is in bed holding the baby.

Daddy helps me climb onto the bed with Mummy. When I join her, she gives me a tight squeeze. "This is your baby sister, Ebony," says Mummy with a big smile as tears ran down her cheeks. I can see she is very happy.

Beaming with love and pride, I look at my new baby sister. She is mine, my very own baby sister. I can't stop smiling. I want to jump up and down and tell everyone. My baby sister is tiny with straight black hair and itsy-bitsy fingers and toes. Her skin isn't black or white; it is light brown just like mine.

Ebony is now looking up at me, and then she begins to cry. Mummy says she needs to be fed, so she breastfeeds her so Ebony will stop crying. Sure enough, Ebony goes quiet.

Everyone's Home

A few days after my baby sister is born, my Daddy brings my Mummy and Ebony home from the hospital. Very quickly I realise that Ebony doesn't do very much. All she does is sleep, eat, cry and poo.

I tell mummy that Ebony isn't much fun. She explains that Ebony is a baby and that babies don't do very much at this stage, except eat and sleep. She reminds me that I need to be patient and tells me that when I was a baby, I was exactly the same.

She opens a drawer and shows me pictures of me when I was a baby. I looked just like Ebony! Mummy tells me I can be a good older brother by helping her with Ebony. I can do things like sing to the baby, help feed Ebony and give Ebony lots of hugs and kisses.

Mummy reminds me that even though she has to spend a lot of time with Ebony, she still loves me very much. I understand that Ebony needs all our help for her to grow big and strong like me. While Mummy is busy helping Ebony grow, I get to spend more time playing with Daddy. I can't wait until Ebony is older so we can play together.

Since Ebony's birth, a lot of people have been visiting. I am very happy to see all our visitors, but I am most excited to see my Grandad and Gran who flew in an airplane all the way from England.

I love spending time with them because I haven't seen them for so long. They are staying with us for three weeks. A few days later, my Daddy's mum and dad also come to visit. Our home is filled to bursting with so much love. Ebony and I get lots of loving hugs and kisses. It reminds me how much I really, really love my family. I hope Mummy has lots more babies, so I can have lots more siblings to play with.

Naomi Kissiedu-Green

Same, but different

This is a story about a boy called Kobi and his family. Kobi is mixed race and there are not many families like Kobi where Kobi lives. Kobi's teacher, with the help of Kobi's parents, shows Kobi and his class that people can appear different, but they also very often have a lot in common. Together Kobi and his classmates learn to accept that everyone is different… but in some respects, they are also the same.

ABOUT THE AUTHOR

I am a wife and mother who relishes bringing my ideas and passion to life.

In my capacity as mother and qualified childcare worker I have been disheartened to discover the paucity of resources that cater to multicultural families in Australia. It can be a struggle to find books to read to your children that depict multicultural families – or even families of other cultures. I honestly wish there were more representations of cultures and mixed race people in the media.

So I wrote this book for multiracial families like mine, and other families who want to embrace diversity and acceptance. It's important for children to see themselves as they develop a sense of community and belonging. It is our responsibility – as parents and as a nation – to make children feel included not just in their home, but in the classroom and in life.

Racial and ethnic group differences have a significant impact on children's social development. Although the impact varies according to age and ethnicity, it is important for children to take pride in their heritage.

I hope to shine a spotlight on the issue of mixed race with my Kobi books, and offer something to multiracial families with which they can identify.

Surprise Baby

www.ingramcontent.com/pod-product-compliance
Lightning Source LLC
Chambersburg PA
CBHW061931290426
44113CB00024B/2880